Sunshine over the Monstera Fields

Shivani -

Presentation by *BookLeaf Publishing*

Web: www.bookleafpub.com

E-mail: info@bookleafpub.com

ISBN:9789358730302

First edition 2023

DEDICATION

To those who spread happiness evenhanded to all, even if they may not be receiving as much.

To your braveness and kindness.

To your struggles and victories.

ACKNOWLEDGEMENT

For this beautiful life full of adventures and love, I am thankful to my mother, my biggest inspiration and support.

For making this book possible thanks to all those who stood beside me and told me to do it anyway, even when I had massive doubts.

For believing in me and pushing me, I thank my sister who has been my unpaid therapist, critic, and lifeline throughout.

PREFACE

When her pen slipt out of her fingers
reality struck too hard,
For she was about to make miracles
when caught off guard.

- fear of the lost

Hopeless Notions of Love

The moment you find it,
You know somewhere
You will lose it, then why?
Perhaps that smile kept you going.

Waiting for the perfect one
is like waiting for the stars to come down.
Regardless of how hopeless,
We still look up and wait.

Do I have to wake up?
No! Not this dream.
Let me stay for a bit.
Let me sleep a little longer.

All my time is yours is a myth.
Why measure the amount of space
I have for you in my life?
Or that mine ever matter more?

All or Nothing

Afraid to get close,
let us meet in isolation.
Battling our egos,
Let us converse in ignorance.

In the journey to find solice,
Let us pretend happiness
Because nothing may ever
Suffice boundless desperation.

Twisted Parallels

When will it hit you, baby?
When will you come by again?
Will our love stay through the seasons
and keep us warm and safe?

You held me all across the oceans and cities
Held me tight at night.
Haven't you done everything you could?
Maybe it has come to this.

Every other guy who found my world
But you're the only one who discovered the
code.
I see it go away.
I see it perishing.
And those laughs and moans will haunt me
alone.

I'm a kite, so I fly high
But it is time to cut the rope
No, not with another lie.

You see we are stuck in twisted parallels.
Sigh! We can't help it b'cause
we are just lines

drawn around,
Never-ending but never one.

Mercy

Have mercy, dear lord!
Plead the horrible soul for letting its mate go
away.

Grant the glorious freedom
for it has been in glorious pain.

Misery found an unworldly pleasure
in a world where people bow to you.

So, mercy me, mercy the soul,
Pardon this one to save both.

Pushing Boundaries

We just hear the echos of our speech
So we sound different each time.
If I were to receive these words of diminish
I would be thrown off, unable to climb.

But some thrive on them.
the violent screams
Mixed with hints of ecstasy.

They play by the rules
And their superior attitudes.
Not mine but yours
Was the hill I couldn't cross.

Now you claim there is a wall between us
Full of points of pride and tides.
No, it is just the horizon
And I am on the other side.

Unknown Threshold

Maybe time will catch up to memory
Somewhere on the back of my brain
There's an itch that isn't cured fully.

Latched those thoughts where you held close
calls.
I am done with my doze of being hung up
Watching your ghost, my guards take the fall.

Been told a million ways to get through the
rough
and turn worried faces upside down
But never did anyone teach me how to know I
have had enough.

False Awakenings

Shutting my screen
Picking up pieces
Lonely as ever
Went on for seasons.

The noise is gone.
Now you may enter
Dreams are for the rich
Or maybe I just let her.

Into my bones,
Into my soul,
Easy to anchor her shipwreck
and access control.

What are these visions I am shown?
Buried in tattered pages of my poems.
Enough! now leave my brain
And everything you owned.

Fresh Wound

Bleeding even after those stitches,
My cries weren't enough to stop the flow.

Trying to paint a smile through scares,
My cries never felt like a source.

Buring the wound to cure the pain,
My cries still failed to move you.

Because among the sounds of eight billion
heartbeats,
My cries were just noise for you.

Hold On

To the thought of being a trendsetter
Seeing through imperfections,
Holding on to something better
Than mulling over lost affections.

My to-dos have faded
Among your nightmare and terrors.
My castle was invaded
Counting on my irreversible errors.

I was happy to see you half awake
So, I held you a bit closer that night.
Maybe this one last time before I shake
Off your memories in plain sight.

I could have grown to be a friend
Even as your watchful usher
In your tries to make amends
You ended up making me suffer.

So, as I hold on to your dreadful exist
tears were all I found.
I'm still hoping this won't persist
Holding on to the thoughts I am bound.

Switching Seasons

Wrapped up in my favourite blanket,
I click play on my influential box.
The comfort of biting winds and creaking floors
broads,
Replaced the misfortune and set the clock.

I wear a hoodie that has seen many seasons,
And unseen by several of your looks.
My skin kissed the sun as I gave my goodbyes
I filled all the pages, the journals, and the
notebooks.

Wondering how the frost didn't bite me,
I land on this fateful reality-

Winter doesn't mind me anymore,
the summer has caught up to the chore.
I thought forgetting your ashes would wear me
down.
But you went ahead and scarred my summers
with your relentless love spree.

The story continues, but the players have
changed

Not just the faces, the roles, attitudes, and
everything.

You might have met me here at Paradise,
nothing short of Christmas,
But you ruined light for me, cause that's when
you met her.

Fortune-telling Succulent

What is it with plants
So pretty, engorged, and damp
That they need so little
Still don't flinch to decamp.

The pressure of its care
Nearly pushes your limits
Looking closely for cracks
Feeling almost inhibited.

Then the winter came fast,
Freezing the plump leaves
Now, it's indoors for you,
Off the icy winds and thieves.

All this while
How daft I have been
Going against nature
Protecting from within.

Vexed, I plead, Why?
Why make me watch it die?
I made all the amends in me
Yet left with no time to buy.

The heat was ample,
The shields were all in place.
Was it the soil with no sand?
That doomed the poor thing's base.

The appalling discovery,
A trick, a prank, or perhaps a quirk?
Since nothing else really can explain
How a fortune-telling succulent works.

Dark Poetry

Reaching for the coffee as I read you again,
Read every corner of you to understand your
functioning,
A thought just sort of struck me.

You are my dark poetry.
Your verse is pure but your intentions are cruel.

Some poetries have darkness as lucidity
But you have no sane intervals,
You exist because you hurt.

The very feature of you is that you say
everything out
Wrapped in the fumes of darkness.

Your humour rips my broken heart.

I reach the part where I long for
a beat from your still, cold heart.

The darkness and melancholy in your words
is somehow romantic and soothing.

Yet your end is as appealing as my fear of your
brightness.

You are my dark poetry,
And I will make sure you are my last.

Note of Thanks

Thanks to the one that got away
with more than just my temper.
Thanks for teaching me not to ever love again.

Gratitude came rushing as I recall
how brilliantly you described my love
as tenacious, well, you were so right.

You won my heart all over
when you said how I just had you
to treat my day and end my night.

I might have just fallen for you again
when you amusingly wiped my tears
just to tell me I had fallen in front of you.

My tears were completely worthless.
And the way you made me laugh at myself was
just award-winning.

All this time you were right and I couldn't see
through my blind, horrible, insane pair of eyes.

Thank you for filtering all the cruelty and giving
me what I wanted, pity.

So, I bend my knees, and as I cross my heart,
I think of every brain wrecking thought you put
in my head
and plead for mercy from your existence.

Thank you for letting me down
and sorry for not smiling
every time you made me feel thankful.

Afterthought

Months of grief and tears later,
there I was among your chaotic thoughts.
Obscure as it may seem, a fanatic entry indeed
It was of the long-lost pitiful affliction.

I hear from your friends and you hear from ours
That oh! well, you made it across the shore
Dumping my shells in the water,
All without a boat or even a soul.

Your hurray' lasted for exactly one heartbreak
And came gushing back like the waves.
Forgetful of your predictability, I get curious,
Don't be expecting the skies, you live in a cave, I
tell myself.

Like after the courteous dinner comes the
gratitude
Or the applause that comes after the end credits,
I came in sheepishly, bashfully, to your
consciousness
Not a wildcard, not even a mate but just as an
afterthought.

One of those times when your inner self screams
'I told you so'
A sigh escapes your lips and your heart stiffens.
Rest in peace, o superficial expectations,
Life has its way of making sure the plot
thickens.

A Vile Valentine

I feel like I have to write,
Pour out my unquenched heart.
Did I flee or put up a fight?
Its too late for me to skip this part.

Based on what we know,
Go for careful affections.
Hear your heart but not when its low,
Even if it means following aimless directions.

Oh! almighty dependence,
Can't you see I am drained?
While hurt came in abundance,
Love didn't make it, it failed.

A macabre turn of events,
Led to this calculated fiasco.
Every time I brood it's explication
I end up discovering a new low.

Your victory in ripping my faith
Was by holding my head down in endless hope.
So, tell me, in this perfect misery you create,
Do we hold ground or give in to the slippery
slope?

Old Roads

Cut me into small pieces
And bury me when I arrive
Cause those old roads
Are not to blame
For things that were once mine.

The streets run cold
As I walk alone in the sun.
My head hurts
Under the scorching heat but
My heart believed you were in one.

The one who painted
Her echoes all over the city.
Now I'm running behind memories
Like I was running behind you
Thinking our old roads will exist in theory.

Those endless arrays of food
They have started to rot,
Standing in lines for you,
I got your favorites things
Even when you said it was a lot.

You said this place would

Only remind you of us and our ways
Yet you were so unhinged
That you went to the extent
Of making me bear witness to this day.

Small Emotions

Can emotions be so small?
Negligible and overlooked?

How dare you stoop down and say
I am not meant to feel what I feel.

Nevertheless, your hurt is deceiving,
Careless and a burden I carry around.

Emotions are bottomless
Just like your anguish.

Tiny drops make an oceans
Yet my heart catered to all your motions.

I say goodbye to how
Less I cared about myself.

Trying to make magic
We ended up making a tragedy.

So, like you belittled my problems,
Watch me belittle your memory.

From the Outside

For any good left in you,
Sorry, it will end badly.
But if you thrive on toxicity,
It won't end, for all of eternity.

I can see it.
Why can't you?
Maybe because you hide in the closet,
While I now blissfully enjoy the view.

From the outside,
It seems so incredibly stupid
To have stayed more than I did.

From the outside,
It makes so much sense
For you to have missed the Cupid.

From the outside,
I now know there was good in me,
and none in you.

From the outside,
It ended for me,
But would never for you.

Imitating Seasons

Being with me is like living in a movie
Everyone likes it there but leaves when the show
is over.

Thus, in a world of imitating the wanted,
How do you get to keep what's yours?

So, it is fine if you act the part out,
turn on the false meter of smiling while you are
on the clock.

These are imitating seasons, dear friend
You better do your dance and hope some stay till
your epilogue.

Healing- Behind the Scenes

Dare to wonder
If knowing spoils the fun
Need we consider
The repercussions of an endless dump.

It's like you watch yourself fall
In great detail, the paths we crossed.
Maybe even with a pinch of salt
Extracted from the oceans of fault.

You glide through pain & hurt with no fear,
Exaggerated changes and diabolical thoughts.
You pass by the past, numb as your heart
Yet who would believe Miss Goldilocks?

The replay of the journey leads
To an outburst of profanity
The night's more clear
Than any of your pretend clarity.

Die slowly,
But do sure leave
The captured ground,
Once a heart of steal.

Regret wrapped in anger
Is one timeless bitch
Peaking through the fixes,
Revealing every bait and switch.

Healing comes easy
Tough thoughts wiped clean.
A brave smile to fool the world
When none know the plot behind the scenes.

Verse on a paperback

Under the blanket,
Beneath the torchlight,
I found some company in words
And a friend to spend the night.

I wandered away for a long time.
How could words set you free?
Heedless of my time left in exile,
I pick one up to find the old me.

The pain in the pages
They reattached my shattered heart.
The smell of newly printed leaves
Put me to sleep short of your depart.

Some pages took in my tears,
Some ensured I wasn't anywhere near reality,
Some even made me feel close to you,
Well, some spoke of your shameless duality.

Every time I picked one up,
It almost felt like you knew
That maybe refining my taste
Would somehow bring me back to you.

Now I embark on journeys more than a few
Oblivious of whether it is hitting you enough,
Pinching you just right to decide
If you literally or literary left me rough.

I fathomed you'd be a worm
And I, the watchful reciter,
Of our tale of fatal accidents,
Big fat lies and how they got whiter.

Every playful insult,
And every intentional offend,
Pierced through my broken heart
Wishing for its keeper to defend.

Well, I don't blame you for stopping at my cover
Missing out on my contents and prelude
Now look at me finish my climax,
Unaffected by our invisible feud.